It was the fourth day of their holiday in Rome. Robin and Marta were tired of keeping up with their aunt and uncle's frenetic pace. Aunt Franca had made an elaborate plan to visit all the churches, monuments, buildings and museums in Rome in one week. It's impossible, but she was doing her best! They had already been in two churches and a museum that day and it was now lunchtime.

Auntie had planned a picnic on the Appian Way and Robin and Marta were exhausted.

A month earlier, when aunt Franca had told them they could come for an "educational" week with her and uncle Adrian, they had been delighted. And in actual fact it would have been great if auntie hadn't always been reading, from a big book, long pages of comments on everything they saw. Uncle Adrian just muttered: he looked tired and distraught. A week like this was exhausting for him too, as he usually only sat at his desk…

Auntie's sandwiches disappear in a flash. Uncle mutters something and lies down under a big cypress tree. Auntie starts to read.
Robin wants to play but Marta doesn't. She's a bit disappointed about the holiday; maybe it would have been better to stay at home. There's her tennis lesson and Mirella, her best friend, is having a party this week. But then, when she thinks of her friends sitting in the classroom, she feels like laughing; after all it's not all that bad being here in Rome. Completely lost in her thoughts, Marta takes some time before she realises that Robin is calling her. What does he want to get up to this time? Robin has a weakness for hiding places and Marta bets he wants to go into that hole.

Come here Marta! There's a staircase!

Yes, okay, I'm coming!

The monk, when he hears Marta's apology, regrets being angry. After all they have done nothing wrong and it is nice for him to speak in his own language. Marta knows very well they shouldn't stay there, but she's really curious: she's happy too because the monk isn't shouting anymore.

Please excuse me young lady, don't go yet, I've got an idea. My name is Brother Sebastian, I come from Ireland but I live in a monastery near here and you have just discovered my secret mushrooms. These mushrooms have to grow in the dark so as to stay white and the catacombs are the ideal place for growing them. But do you know what the catacombs are? I've got a very special passage in here, just come with me and I'll show you the catacombs.

Yes, but we can come with you only for a little while; we have to go back soon because our aunt and uncle are waiting for us outside on the grass. My name is Marta.

And I'm Robin.

Brother Sebastian takes a big rusty key and opens the heavy door at the end of his secret room. He asks Marta and Robin to follow him. Behind the door there's a narrow corridor which runs into another one a few steps further down.

Here we are in the catacombs; that's how these underground passages are called. A long time ago they were used as a Christian cemetery. Just think, there are so many of these passages that you can walk for hours. In all there are almost 100 kilometres of them under Rome. Can you see your brother, Marta? You'd better follow him. Never lose sight of each other. Don't be afraid as there's so much to learn and it'll only take a couple of minutes.

Marta starts to run: she wants to stay near Robin, who tends to disappear all the time behind some corner. They go right, left, then up and down stairs, and after a while they have completely lost their bearings. They don't know where they are. Only passages. An enormous underground labyrinth. After some more corridors, there is a change. Marta realises that many of the niches are closed by a stone slab, and that there are drawings or writings on these slabs. And then there are some small glass vases, and lanterns, lit here and there, emanating a soft glow.

Robin, I'm afraid we are lost, we have to find a way out.
My head is spinning. Can you smell the stench of perfume, too?

Look Marta, there's a light moving at the end of the corridor!

Robin and Marta run towards the light. The room at the end of the corridor is painted all in white, and there are figures and coloured lines. Many oil lamps are hanging in front of the marble slabs which have symbols and names inscribed on them. But the strangest thing is that Brother Sebastian is standing in the middle of the room with a white sheet draped around him, looking like an old Roman character. Marta is about to laugh, but the Brother is terribly serious and starts to tell a story…

You are laughing at my robe, Marta, but I am dressed normally for these times. Entering through my door you have gone back in time to the Roman age, and now you can come with me to see what it was like. Among the many tombs of common people there are also some special ones. In this room there are the tombs of the Popes. Then there are those of the martyrs. Every now and then Christians come here to the catacombs to commemorate and pray on their tombs. Today, though, I can't see a living soul; come on and have a look outside.

Oh, thank goodness it's quiet today. We are in the cemetery of St. Callistus, who was the director of this place for twenty years before becoming Pope. The third century, which we will briefly visit, is not always as calm as it looks today. In these hundred years all sorts of things have happened, and there have also been terrible persecutions of the Christians. Decius, for instance, one of the many emperors of this stormy age, compels the Christians to sacrifice an animal or to pour oil on some pagan altar. The river is red from the blood of the animals, but many Christians refuse to make these sacrifices so as not to betray their religion. The ones who don't obey are condemned to death. The Christians who die in this way are called martyrs.

Along all the roads leading out of Rome there are monuments and tombs to commemorate the dead. Rich families have mausoleums, which are tombs as big as castles. This is the Appian Way, which goes to Brindisi in the south of Italy. All the ships coming from Greece dock there. The Appian Way is so important that it is called Regina Viarum, the Queen of the Roads.

Outside St. Callistus' cemetery, Brother Sebastian helps the children onto a pretty cart pulled by an ox. There is a lot of traffic on the road: there are carts, little ones and big ones, all full of goods, and people on foot or on horse-back... Robin looks around him and thinks how different it all is; it is like being in a film.

Brother Sebastian takes the children with him along the Via Sacra, the street that crosses the Roman Forum, which is the main square in Rome.

Look at how many temples and altars! The Romans worship many different Gods: Minerva, Apollo, Saturn, Mars or Jupiter, and also foreign Gods, like Isis, who comes from Egypt, or Mithras, who is Persian. Generally the Romans leave everybody free to worship the God one wants, and that is why there are so many sanctuaries. But, besides their personal cult, everybody must take part in the cult of the Roman State. This is something the Christians cannot accept. More and more people now believe in the Gospel, the message of Jesus, and this rapid growth is frightening the emperors.

Yes, they are, because the Christians obey the emperor only if his rules don't conflict with their faith.

Are they scared?

As soon as they arrive near the temple of Mars, the Roman God of war, they see a terrible sight. Brother Sebastian tells them that it is a sacrifice to the Gods, a ceremony with a very difficult name: suovetaurilia. It means that it is a sacrifice of a sus, a pig, of an ovis, that is a ram, and a taurus, which is a bull. It is a ritual to appease the bloodthirsty Gods of the sky, the earth and the underworld. These poor animals are killed just there in front of the temple while all the people in the square echo the sharp sound of the trumpets with shouts and clapping. Marta is about to be sick and Brother Sebastian comments: Pagans!

Robin is very interested in the show. He tries to get through the pushing crowd to reach the podium. He would like to climb up there, but a soldier stops him. It is forbidden. Robin turns round to go back to Marta, but before he manages to spot her someone lifts him up and hurriedly takes him away.

For the whole journey Robin can see hardly anything, because the man who is taking him away has hung him upside down over his shoulders like a sack of potatoes. When Robin is finally put down and looks around, he sees these three figures in front of him. The man doesn't look very kind and the boys have very sad faces. All three of them stare at Robin, who blushes and feels very uneasy.

Yes, I think that this boy can be suitable, he looks intelligent, and even has red hair, which is uncommon, and it can be an asset. I'll keep him hidden at home and then tomorrow I'll sell him in the slave market!

Ave, my name is Caius. I've been told that you've got lost. Poor boy. They have brought you here to my house so that you can play with my sons while we look for your family. Don't worry, nothing bad will happen to you. Come, I'll show you the atrium where you can wait until your family comes to get you.

Look what a funny boy, he looks like a carrot with that hair; and look at his clothes, who knows where he comes from.

I am not going to play with someone like him! I hope dad sells him for a lot of money, so he'll buy me a new ball.

In the roof of the big room where Robin is waiting there is an opening called impluvium; at least that's what the man said when Robin asked why it was there. Its purpose is to collect the rain in the basin in the middle. Just five minutes later the man leaves Robin alone with the boys, but they disappear behind a curtain instead of playing. Robin looks around for a while: the room is very beautiful, and is full of marble and bronze statues. Then his curiosity gets the better of him and he looks inside one of the other rooms…

In the room Robin sees three ladies sitting at a table; actually they look more like witches than ladies. In the air there is a strange smell of incense. Even if Robin would have liked to go away, he feels like he is being pushed towards the women by an invisible hand.

The old witch has locked Robin in the cellar. Everything in this villa is spacious, even the storeroom is large and full of big amphoras. In the floor there is the opening of a huge jar. Robin moves the heavy marble lid. He finds a ladle and pulls it up and tastes the contents. It's wine! After having looked everywhere Robin sits down and starts to get worried: why doesn't Marta come and rescue me? And what if nobody is looking for me? And if that witch comes back what will she do to me? No, it's better if I think that nothing is real and that it is only a strange dream… What will happen?

Marta and Brother Sebastian are looking for Robin everywhere. They ask people in the streets if they have seen a red-haired boy, and soon somebody points at the road towards the villa. The man who steals children is well known and hasn't got many friends in the neighbourhood. Near the villa they meet a girl. Her name is Anna, and she tells them that she, together with Andreas, who is a slave in the villa, has a plan to free Robin.

Go into the third house in the next street on the left and you'll find a church on the first floor. You have to wait for Andreas there. He'll be there as soon as possible.

In the meantime Robin is feeling lonelier and lonelier. He is almost on the point of bursting into tears when suddenly a very kind boy enters the room. The boy helps him into a big wicker basket, which he loads onto his wide shoulders. Luckily Robin is not heavy!

Don't worry boy, we are Christians too, and we always try to help each other. The witches are wicked and the master of the house is a famous thief. Unfortunately we, who are slaves in this house, cannot free ourselves but now that we have our faith we feel free anyway. I'll take you away from here, so you can find your father and your sister!

He's not my father, but thanks for taking me away. Are you sure the witches won't notice?

You see, there is a big difference between a temple and a church. Pagan temples are kept closed, only the priests can go in, and the sacrifices are made on an altar in front of the temple.
The church instead is like a home, where the faithful meet together to hear the Gospel. The bishop sits on the throne and explains the words of God. The other clerics sit around him and the faithful sit in front of the altar, but only those baptised can remain for the communion. The Baptism is held only once a year on Easter night...

Interesting, but... aren't you worried about Robin?

Marta and Brother Sebastian are in the church waiting for Robin. It's a big room and nothing can be seen from the outside. But, once inside, one can immediately understand it is a church, as Christian symbols are painted on the walls and there is an altar, a big throne for the bishop and the benches for the community.

So now it's getting time to go away from here. There is a long corridor behind this little door, which will take you back to the catacombs. Keep going straight on and you'll come to the stairs where you came in. You'll see that very little time has gone by. What you have seen and heard is just one of the many pleasant and unpleasant facts one has to learn. Past history is part of our life and it is right to get to know our roots, don't you agree?

Yes, we have seen so much! Everything seems strange and complicated now; I'll have to think it over for a long time. Thank you Brother Sebastian, and goodbye!

I'm happy to go, at least the witches won't find me!